BRITAIN IN OLD PH(

OTLEY & DISTRICT

PAUL WOOD

ALAN SUTTON PUBLISHING LIMITED

Alan Sutton Publishing Limited
Phoenix Mill · Far Thrupp · Stroud
Gloucestershire · GL5 2BU

First published 1995

Cover photographs: (front) Kirkgate, Otley, c. 1905; (back) motor charabanc, 1920s.

British Library Cataloguing in Publication Data.
A catalogue record for this book is available from the British Library.

ISBN 0-7509-1010-0

Typeset in 9/10 Sabon.
Typesetting and origination by
Alan Sutton Publishing Limited.
Printed in Great Britain by
WBC Ltd, Bridgend.

Dedicated to Christine for her love, affection, intelligence and cataloguing.

Otley Museum, Civic Centre, (The Mechanics),
Cross Green, Otley, West Yorkshire, England.
Hon. Keeper, Paul Wood, 5 Garnett Street, Otley.
Reg. Charity 519264

Otley Museum holds a comprehensive collection of objects, artefacts and documentary material relating to the development of Otley and district since the prehistoric period. The museum is managed entirely on a voluntary basis, acting as a central point at which historical resources can be conserved, recorded and interpreted for the benefit of public education.

Tel. 01943 461052 Monday, Tuesday, Friday mornings for enquiries.

Contents

Bay Horse Yard, *c.* 1930. Otley is a plain stone-built market town with a strong vernacular architectural tradition. The town centre buildings, primarily of the eighteenth and nineteenth centuries, were built on a thirteenth-century street plan. Bay Horse Yard squeezes its narrow ginnel access to the Market Place between the medieval burgage plots.

Introduction

Otley and District in Old Photographs is a further opportunity to bring the wonderful collection in Otley Museum into the public gaze. The compilation of this book not only reveals new pictorial images for simple enjoyment, but also extends the range of educational material produced by the museum for the detailed study of the community.

While the camera shows new views of town life from the late nineteenth century, there are other glimpses of Wharfedale and the Washburn valley. The photographers' lenses reflect the museum's actual collecting policy for the ancient townships of the parish and the obvious social connections with the middle Wharfe valley. The Washburn watershed extends this five-mile radius north because of its parallel tributary links. The historical development of the area, seen through these topographical photographs, spans some three score years and ten from around 1880 to the middle of the twentieth century.

At the beginning of the period we still see an ancient market town amid a famously beautiful valley, despite the burgeoning industrial expansion of the 'Wharfedale' printers' engineers. Bustling streets provide services for locals and market-day farmers. Butcher, grocer and maker of candles rub shoulders with blacksmith, ropemaker and sweep. Remnants of the old manorial town remain in form and custom and the eighteenth-century core is punctuated by a new Victorian façade. The pillars, pediments and pinnacles of the nineteenth century are seen in institute, school and Gothic villa. The succeeding years see the development of local government planning and the expansion of surburban public housing, all interrupted by the upheavals of war.

In the surrounding green fields of Wharfedale a rural tradition is dominated by the demands of the landed estate, its paternal culture and the ever-watchful eye of the gamekeeper. The private peace is periodically shattered by turnpike, railway navvy and military encampment.

The Washburn valley shows the last vestiges of an upland farming landscape turned into a fossilised lake district by the city of Leeds reservoirs.

The photographers range from the locally renowned to the unknown, using either unwieldly apparatus or a casual snapshot camera. Fading and damaged prints may reduce the clarity of our view, but cannot dim our fascination for the choice of subject. In a late twentieth century of bewildering change we seek a stability in sepia streets, poetic portraits and lingering landscapes.

Paul Wood
May 1995

Lindley Bridge, Washburn valley, *c.* 1905. Carrying the old road from Otley to Harrogate, the eighteenth-century bridge was improved for traffic by Thomas Clifton in 1808. Turner, the landscape artist, paused here in 1818 to record an exaggerated alpine scene of the bridge, with Lindley Hall on the hillside above. The winter beauty of the Wharfe's tributary river is photographed by William Weegmann of Otley.

Section One

OTLEY

Otley Bridge, c. *1880. This magnificent stone span enabled early exploitation of the manorial estates of Newall, Northwood and Swinsty, and also contact with the Washburn valley. The medieval bridge with five central ribbed arches was partially repaired after the flood of 1673 and substantially rebuilt in 1775.*

The Navvies memorial, Otley churchyard, *c.* 1890. This replica of the northern portal of the Bramhope tunnel on the Leeds to Thirsk line was erected to commemorate the navvies who lost their lives building the railway between 1845 and 1849. The soft Caen stone original pictured here was eventually replaced with local material. A slate panel quotes St Luke in a crushing reference to the victims 'upon whom the Tower of Siloam fell'. Elizabeth Garnett, the navvy missionary, was the daughter of the Revd Joshua Hart, Vicar of Otley, and grew up with her father's deep concern for the welfare of this migrant workforce.

'Whistling' Albert Walker, the spirit of Victorian Otley. The son of William Walker, printer and publisher, Albert was novelist, playwright, poet, wit and doyen of the musical soirée. His whistling recitals were legendary, be they accompanied by his brother William, principal violin in the Hallé Orchestra, or an impromptu performance of 'The Last Rose of Summer' under the Buttercross in the Market Place.

Otley from the Chevin, May 1887. A spring day in late Victorian Otley is captured on a plate camera with panoramic exposures of up to 8 seconds. A contemporary word picture explains: 'printing, tanning and leather dressing and printing machine making are carried on here, the latter business has become one of the principal trades, and is one for which the town bears considerable repute.' In the foreground the railway sidings

are packed with wagons. To the west of Gay Lane, Elliott's Steel Croft machine works is under construction giving employment to workers of the adjoining terraces. The undeveloped acres of Newall-with-Clifton stretch to the moorland horizons of the Washburn valley.

The Buttercross, Market Place, shortly before the building of the Jubilee clock in 1888. Richard Coad the watchmaker and Thomas Lockwood the druggist trade from the Old Hall. Mounsey the stationer and Friendship the ironmonger are to their right. Beyond the butcher's shop is Thomas Rhodes, tallow chandler and candle maker.

Market Place, *c.* 1905. A century earlier the butchers' shambles here were described as a disgrace to Otley: 'a few old buildings, both trifling and inconvenient, should be suffered to occupy the middle of its market place.' New civic pride was displayed with the erection of the Jubilee clock in 1888.

The architect, Alfred Marshall, 1850–1932. The son of Thomas Forrest Marshall of Burras House, he had a significant influence on the public face of Otley. His first designs for the Springsyde villas on Birdcage Walk in 1866 were followed by the familiar Board School, Liberal Club, Jubilee clock, Infant School and Mechanics' Art School. His housing continues to support life at Guy Croft, Fern Bank and Richmond Terrace, and his architecture still provides shelter for Otley Museum a hundred years later.

The celebrations for the coronation of Edward VII were delayed for six weeks by the king's appendicitis operation, but finally took place on 9 August 1902. At seven minutes past three on the afternoon of the great day the corner of the Market Place declares 'God save the King'.

'Success to agriculture' proclaims the decoration for the 100th anniversary of Otley Show in 1898. The three shops at Nos 4, 6 and 8 Market Place are Mrs Fieldhouse the draper and milliner, Weegmann the pork butcher who had his slaughterhouse behind the shop in Blue Bell Yard, and Milner Jackson the butcher. To the immediate right of these premises was the George Hotel.

Mr Weegmann, the butcher. 'The results of his labours may be seen daily in the tempting displays in the shop window, where the appetising Epicure sausage may make even the dyspeptic feel hungry. The raised pies are just the thing for the visitor who requires a hasty but substantial meal.'

A letter dated 1894 to German immigrant Wilhelm Weegmann from the Daimler Motoren Gesellschaft shows just how close Otley came to the manufacture of the Daimler car. Family friend Daimler encouraged negotiations between Weegmann and Payne & Sons for vehicle production. However, the 'New Petroleum Motor' never made Otley famous – the pork pie did!

Otley Old Hall facing the Market Place, 1906. This fine town house, built by the influential Barker family over two centuries earlier, finally succumbed to Victorian commerce around 1843 when the ground floor was converted into shops. The fashionable headgear of Suttle's outfitters occupies the position of the Barkers' front portico.

A floral hat show for the Nonconformist Whit Monday sing in the Market Place, *c.* 1905. Church school congregations met in Manor Square and both groups promenaded around town in sartorial splendour.

Kirkgate, *c.* 1905. Some of the shops visible on the right-hand side of the street starting at the Jubilee clock are Helliwell's corner shop, the Queen's Head Hotel with the hanging sign, Quilter the draper and silk mercer, Edson the tailor and hosier, Hutton the hatter and draper, and Harry Thornton the jeweller, watchmaker and tobacconist. In the left foreground is the sign of the Red Lion held by Daniel T. Spence. The large building beyond is William Walker & Sons Ltd, printers and publishers of the *Wharfedale Observer* since 1880. The prolific enterprise was founded by 'Printer Walker' in 1811 at the age of sixteen, and was instrumental in employing joiner William Dawson in the development of cutting, ruling and printing machinery. After the death of the proprietor in 1871, the business was run by his equally talented sons, Edmund and Albert. The window shoppers would not recognise the modern Kirkgate ninety years on. Progress has produced danger, pollution and the traditional pedestrian under siege.

William Edmund Turner, iron and steel merchant, ironmonger and founder, Kirkgate, *c.* 1880. Turner moved down the street to purpose-built showrooms facing the Market Place in 1899, prior to the redevelopment of the property next to the church gates as Kirkgate Arcade.

G.W. Brotherton's tailor and outfitter's shop at No. 61 Kirkgate. New plans for larger shop fronts were approved on 4 February 1907.

'Albert' the 1910 proprietorial engine by Pollit & Wigzell of Sowerby Bridge at William Walker & Sons' Victoria Printing Works, Kirkgate.

The aftermath of Walker's fire on 11 June 1904. Ranks of Otley-made William Dawson 'Wharfedale' printing machines are mangled wreckage.

F. Pickering's wools and hosiery shop was in the row of seven houses backing on to Otley churchyard from Kirkgate, which were demolished in 1933. 'The knitting specialists, 77 Kirkgate. Ladies can be well advised to call and inspect Mrs Pickering's work. This is undoubtedly first-class. A small shop doing a large trade.'

Otley Parish Church, *c.* 1903. Matters of concern at the vestry meetings of the time were the repair of the chancel, plans for a new organ, insufficient fire insurance and 'the chimes being silent'.

Joshua Hart, Vicar of Otley, 1837–65. The reverend's rhetoric was published by the local printer, William Walker. Hart's sermon at Farnley in words of one syllable – 'The Barren Fig Tree' – was immediately followed in print in 1839 by 'The Stormy Wind' preached after 'The Dreadful Hurricane'. Webb Millington of Boroughgate published 'The Lamp Put Out' and his Mechanics' Institute lectures on Wharfedale in 1857. In early November 1847 Hart had preached to an overflowing congregation on 'The Uncertainty of Human Life as evinced by the awful catastrophe which recently occurred on the Leeds to Thirsk Railway when two men were crushed to death when an arch collapsed on the viaduct'.

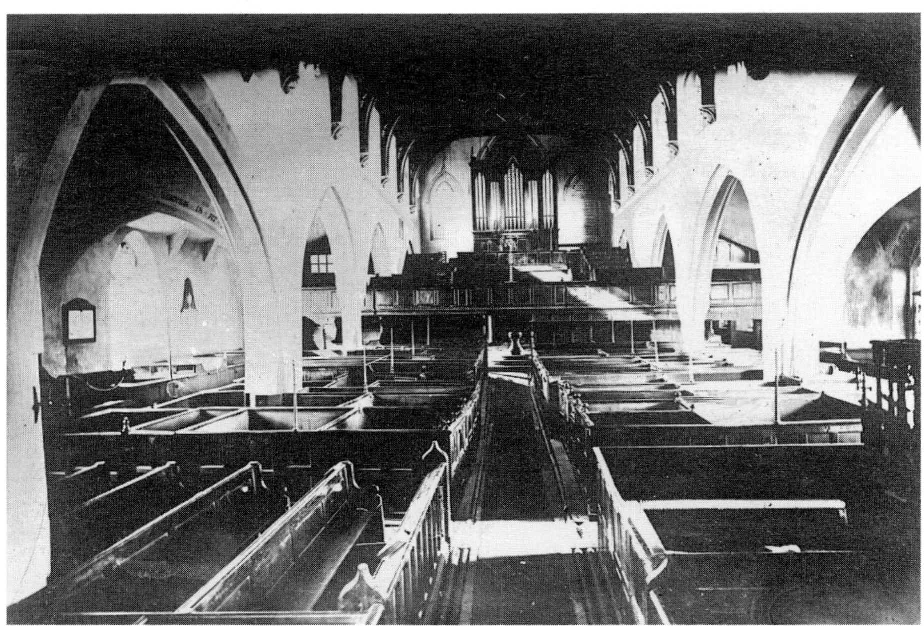

Otley Parish Church interior with its organ, gallery and box pews, before the reopening in 1869 with new seating for 990 people.

Otley Parish Church with the new vestry room to plans by Healey of Bradford, 1890. Frederick Cawood of No. 3 Fairfax Street carried out the building work assisted by his next door neighbour, George Freeman the stone mason.

Otley Parish Church, *c.* 1904. 'Jesus bids us shine with a pure clear light.'

Otley Fire Brigade at the candle works fire, Station Road, 26 November 1954. Tallow-dip candles made from butchers' fats had previously been made in Victoria Yard on the west side of Kirkgate.

The Shand Mason fire-engine at the corner of Weston Lane. This was the second appliance to have the Dawsons of Weston Hall as its patron. The manual engine of 1875 was replaced in 1883 by this latest 'Steamer' which could be coal fired in eight minutes. Capt. Dawson's engine was stored at the hall, and was on offer to the Local Board in times of need.

Bondgate, *c.* 1905. On the left is the Bowling Green Inn held by James Ingham, which was formerly the town's assembly rooms built by Nathaniel Aked in 1757. The upper room, used for concerts and dances, was reached by outside stairs. The building was later adapted as a courthouse, chapel and school. Beyond the cart park is the Walker brothers' Grove House.

James Margerison's rope-making business, Bondgate, 19 August 1936. 'Jimmy' Margerison was a familiar figure at local markets with his range of ropes, nets and halters for the farming community. His rope-walk perfectly utilised the length of one ancient Bondgate croft.

Grove House, Bondgate, *c.* 1902. This was the home of John, Charles and Fred Walker – the family who had long held the old corner grocer's shop on Kirkgate. Their neighbour, William Inman Brockbank of Sugar Street, was the photographer.

The British Restaurant, built on the site of Grove House, served its first public meal on 29 December 1941 in a building supplied by the Ministry of Food. The restaurant not only provided meals on site but also food to works canteens. In 1946 a manageress, seven full-time and eight part-time staff were employed there.

William Hanson, the sweep. Not only did Mr Hanson brush the district's flues, he also became the unlikely subject of family albums and magic lantern shows. This posed portrait appears in Emma Dawson's carte-de-visite album at Weston Hall, and was projected for the entertainment of the town at Charles Walker's 'Old Otley' lectures. George Hanson of Cross Green House swept two chimneys at the Mechanics' Institute on 12 September 1893 for 1*s* each. The Hansons stored soot in a warehouse in their garden.

Jack W. Wood, shoeing and general smith of Crow Lane, *c.* 1936. He was a relation of George and Eric Wood of the Sugar Street forge, whose tools of the trade are displayed in Otley Museum.

William Annison Bull's carriage building works, Gay Lane, *c.* 1925. 'One day's delivery' includes Tordoff's Tea van on the left with a miniature teapot on the bonnet.

Otley Company Home Guard, who were stationed at the Drill Hall, march on Bondgate, October 1940. Harold Walker is second from the right among the marchers.

Gay Lane looking south, *c*. 1905. On the left J. Hardisty provides confectionery and refreshments for cyclists. Beyond the houses on the right stands John Elliott's Steel Croft machine works.

Elliott's improved 'Wharfedale' printing machine, the 'Defiance', made at Gay Lane, *c*. 1893. 'A survey of the whole works, with their exceptional facilities and carefully designed mechanical auxiliaries, conveys some impression of their eminent suitability to the work engaged in – a very model of printing machine engineering.'

The closure of David Payne & Co.'s Caxton Works, Leeds Road, *c.* 1904. Founded in 1892 by John Horner Payne, eldest son of David, the new machine works was born out of brotherly competition at Atlas Works on Burras Lane. Middle row, left to right: Edgar, Percy and Cyril Payne. 'Old Jack' shoulders the breaker's hammer.

Leeds Road looking east, *c.* 1912. The factory chimney on the right marks the site of John Kelley's Albion works, which manufactured 'Wharfedale' printing machines between 1889 and 1905.

James Jefferson, a miner from North Shields, who was charged with the murder of Mrs Elizabeth Todd on Tuesday 5 May 1908. The wife of John Todd the shoemaker of Pool Bank, Mrs Todd had left her home at 4 p.m. that afternoon to walk down Leeds Road to visit her mother in Otley. At 4.10 p.m. Arthur Coates Helliwell, an Otley grocer, witnessed the crime while driving his trap towards the town. Sgt. Herbert Cook later confirmed that he found the prisoner and a woman's body in the field by the road. Despite a plea of insanity, at his trial on 20 July Todd was found guilty of murder and sentenced to death. The sentence was commuted after appeal and Todd spent the rest of his days in an asylum.

Sightseers congregate at the scene of the gruesome crime alongside Holbeck Wood corner on Leeds Road. Elizabeth Todd's murder created a larger crowd outside the Otley courthouse on the morning of Wednesday 6 May 1908. Great public sympathy was shown to the family.

The funeral cortège of Elizabeth Todd moving down Pool Road towards the cemetery on the afternoon of Friday 8 May 1908. Each of Mrs Todd's three children carried flowers to the graveside, and the Otley police formed a protective ring around the family's private grief.

Summer Cross Hotel, Pool Road, *c.* 1889. Thomas Walker is offering billiards and good stabling. During the 1870s the hostelry had capitalised on its position on the Tadcaster Road turnpike, facing Low Bar, but the new hotel turned the property back to front.

The Summer Cross Hotel back garden, *c.* 1889. The Hartleys, gardeners and seedsmen, held closes at Summer Cross, with Samuel Hartley using the triangular fields bordering East Busk Lane as a market garden during the mid-nineteenth century. In 1841 this was Hartley's 'Dwelling house lately erected'.

Wharfedale Agricultural Society's Show, Friday and Saturday, 3 and 4 May 1912. Show day, and all Otley eyes turn to the weather!

The cricketer 'Henry Daphne at the age of 21, father of Jese Daphne and son of William Daphne', *c.* 1880. Far from the field of play, Daphne is posed against an incongruous lakeside backdrop at the studio of William Barraclough on Beech Hill. Richard Burley, glazier of Beech Hill, had almost an annual contract with Cross Green Eleven in the late 1890s. On 1 August 1898 he charged Otley Cricket Club 3*s* 6*d* for '1 pane of Glass put in Wesleyan Minister House, Broken in Play'. The whole smashing process was repeated the following year with exactly the same victim.

Solicitor's Eleven in the Solicitors v. Police cricket match, 27 June 1894. Back row, left to right: Jos. Mason (umpire), R. Forrest, -?-, J. Gledstone, Geo. Cragg (scorer), H. Child, H. Holmes, ? Parrot (umpire), E. Fletcher. Front row: C. Shearsmith, F. Coupland, F. Mudd, C.V. Newstead (captain), J. Morfitt, E.C. Newstead.

The Bremner Machine Company Ltd, Printers' Engineers, Wharfedale Iron Works, *c.* 1897. 'All castings required are made in a foundry on the premises.'

The Bremner Machine, *c.* 1896. 'It embodies numerous improvements, [which] combined with its great compactness, simplicity, and ease of manipulation, have made it a great favourite everywhere, the manufacturers doing a very large home and export trade.'

Otley Mechanics' Institute, *c.* 1890. Completed in 1871 at a cost of about £4,000, it was described as being in 'the modern Italian style' with a library of 3,600 volumes and a large concert hall seating around 800 people. On the ground floor was a lecture room for 250 where science and art classes were held on four nights each week. Originally using Salem Chapel on Bridge Street, members later adapted the old Wesleyan chapel on Nelson Street before moving to the new institute in Cross Green. Designed by Charles Fowler of Leeds, the mason builders were Fleshers of Burley using stone quarried at Pool Bank. The iron fence was a product of Guy Croft Iron Works and later would be a war casualty of the 'Give your railings to the nation' campaign.

Directors of the Otley Mechanics' Institute, 1894. Back row, left to right: G. Farrand, W. Dibb, F.T. Hunter, E.C. Newstead, F. Gill, C. Siddall (Secretary), T.J. Brennan, F.W. Musgrave, C.W. Brown, W. Weegmann, J. Edson. Front row: J. Gledstone, A. Longfield (Vice-President), H.J. Newstead (Vice-President), J.D. Brown (Vice-President), J. Crossfield. The fund-raising for the new Science and Art Schools of the institute was focused on the 'Model Village' Exhibition during August and September 1894 when the old institute was adorned from top to bottom with rural cameos. The cornerstone of the new extension was laid by Mrs Fawkes of Farnley Hall on 29 June 1895. Otley Museum is located in the painting and art master's rooms and holds the comprehensive Mechanics' Institute archive of reports, minute books, diaries, posters and annual accounts from 1834 to 1957.

Cross Green, mid-nineteenth century. Albert Walker's novel *The Rose of Wharfedale* describes celebrations here on May Day 1811. In 1871 the pole was struck by lightning, bombarding the new Mechanics' Institute opposite.

Children at the maypole, *c.* 1907. Speaking of his childhood here in the 1850s, the Revd G.H. Brown commented: 'We boys might whip our tops from one end of Boroughgate to another and no one would say us nay.'

Wharfe Street National Infants' School, 1891.

Ben and Sarah Hollings of No. 36 Cross Green. Benjamin was a builder and mason who erected Otley's new maypole in 1872, and in 1881 offered the services of 'Roger', a good Middle-bred boar.

Bryan Smith standing in the doorway of his grocer's shop at No. 20 Walkergate, *c.* 1900. Stock in trade included Watson's Matchless Cleanser: 'The best soap for all purposes', and Brooke Bond Tea. Fry's Chocolate had 300 gold medals and was by Royal Appointment. The sweet contents of his shop window jars might stop the passing pupils of the Cross Green National Schools. W.H. Edwards, Otley station signalman, also pauses for the photographer.

Peter Patrick's, timber merchants of Wharfedale Saw Mills, Courthouse Street, proudly display their 8 ton 'Heart of Oak'. Founded in 1870, Patrick's made gates, seats and fencing, and supplied more refined orders such as panelling for the *Queen Mary* made from Weston Hall estate sycamore. History does not record the quality of Peter Patrick's wooden leg!

The Otley Building Society offices in Wesley Street looking back towards earlier premises, *c.* 1948. The society's transactions are typified by Surrender of July 1867 when Jeremiah Dawson was advanced £22 *7s 6d* to build a house on a garden called North Burrows above Otley church. Dawson's home was to be on the biblical Mount Pisgah from which Moses viewed the promised land.

Otley's character recorded at the junction of Boroughgate and Market Place in 1971. The author's photographic and architectural surveys, undertaken on behalf of Otley's Outstanding Conservation Area, are held in the museum.

Boroughgate with Hodgson's draper's shop awning on the left, 1910. 'This gives you an idea of the streets here', writes the correspondent.

James Tempest displays his prize carcasses on Boroughgate, *c.* 1909. The transition between market stall, booth and shop is clearly displayed.

Farnley Hall foxhounds at the Royal White Horse, *c.* 1909. The Newall Hall otter-hounds of T.C. Wilkinson hunted the Wharfe, and on 10 June 1902 an observer recorded that an otter was killed 'amid much excitement'.

VE Day is declared from the Royal White Horse, Manor Square, 8 May 1945. The war years in Wharfedale bring memories of ration books, dig for victory and the Home Guard. Grim listings in the *Wharfedale Observer* of men dead, missing and wounded were read by their mothers, wives and sweethearts while toiling on incessant munition tool production at the Otley machine works.

The old grammar school, Manor Square, *c.* 1904. Henry Dacre, solicitor of Manor Offices, carried on his function as Deputy Steward of the Archbishops' Manor of Otley. Beyond is the Craven Bank and the Royal Oak.

Fairfax Fearnley's chemist shop in Manor Square, *c.* 1908. Fearnley had succeeded the druggist business of Richard Pratt, formed in 1854. Pratt's Victorian pills, potions and physic make riveting reading in the museum's collection of six daybooks containing nearly 8,000 prescriptions.

Manor House, the home of Thomas Constable, *c.* 1880. With the site of the York Archbishops' medieval manor house lying to the north-west, this is its secular successor, built by Matthew Wilson in 1784. Attorney Wilson was followed by lawyers Smith and Constable. On the right is the Roman Catholic church built by Constable in his own grounds in 1851.

Aldridge and Dinsdale, gardeners to the Manor House, *c.* 1910. After the death of Thomas Constable in 1891, his wife survived him at the house until 1919. Their only daughter, Mary, had married Baron Mowbray and Stourton in 1893, returning from Allerton Park on her husband's death in 1936. Meanwhile, the house had been occupied by Thomas Andrew Corry. Lady Mowbray and Stourton died here in December 1961, aged 91. Her daughter, the Hon. Charlotte, lived on in the house until its conversion into flats in the late 1970s, her move to Harrogate severing a Constable connection of 140 years.

Manor House Derby Club, 1932. The long-running story of Otley Derby Sweepstake reached its final chapter here in 1932. The brainchild of Archie Britton in 1922, the first lottery was promoted from the Otley Unionist Club. In 1927 Britton had emerged again with the Otley Bowling Supporters' Club and, after a police raid on his offices, summonses were issued for running an illegal lottery. Britton was found guilty and bound over for three years. March 1932 saw a Derby Club tenancy of the Manor House with Lady Mowbray and Stourton as chairman and Mr Britton as managing director. There was talk of a million members and a sweep draw down a mine shaft, on a Scottish express train or up in an airliner! Alas, on 24 May 1932, police made nineteen arrests at the Manor House under the Gaming Act. £500 fines on five directors followed, with an auction of Derby Club effects and its winding up in 1933. With vast sums of money staked on the National Lottery in 1995, perhaps the visionary Archie Britton deserves a statue here next to Thomas Chippendale!

The rebuilding of the Three Horse Shoes adjoining Walter Thompson's smithy, Bridge Street, *c.* 1874. The builder carefully conserved the seventeenth-century mullion windows in the old house and reinserted them in the back wall. The inn was to benefit greatly from trade brought by the removal of the cattle market from Manor Square to the Licks in 1885. Later, landlord Tom Moorhouse advertised stabling for forty horses and stalls for seventy head of cattle. 'Salesmen visiting the market should make this hotel their headquarters.'

Bridge Street, *c.* 1896. On the right is the old Salem Chapel replaced in 1899 by the new church, and on the left are the Sunday schools of 1882. The early congregation of Independents was marked both by their Scottish ancestry and by their trade as travelling merchants and dealers. Facing the chapel across Bridge Street was the Irish immigrant flock at the 1851 Catholic church, who had been dispossessed by the potato famine.

Edwin Smith, Master of the Board Schools, and pupils, *c.* 1879. The Board School opened on 14 January 1878 in the temporary Sunday school classroom at the rear of Salem Chapel, where this group is probably posed. 'Children photographed in the afternoon' records the logbook on 30 June 1879. Smith left the school in 1917.

The Congregational church and North Parade Board Schools form a Victorian backdrop to the lorry fleet of Elisha Dodgshon & Sons, corn and flour dealers of Manor Square, *c.* 1928. 'Try our Bloom rations for cattle and pigs.'

Bridge End and Newall Hall, *c.* 1880. An early nineteenth-century writer had said: 'When the labours of the week are finished, the favourite promenade of the town on Sunday in summer, is down to the bridge, and on the north bank of the river. The placid tranquillity and silver clearness of the river, the view of the noble mansions and distant prospect of green woods and craggy mountains, all here conspire to give refreshment to the weary labourer and peace to the troubled soul.'

The bridge and Bridge Avenue, *c.* 1910. 'On the lower side are the pavilions of the Otley Swimming and Life Saving Society. Visitors are allowed to have use of the rooms on payment of 4d., for which sum they are provided with costume and towels. Apply to F. Thurlby, Bridge Avenue.'

Wharfeside Mills, *c.* 1908. Peter Garnett & Son, paper makers with Harry Garnett at Wharfeside House were based here. The manager was R.A. Barton, and Albert Young was the chauffeur at Gate House.

Riverdale Villas, *c.* 1900. William Robinson, grocer of Boroughgate, reclines in front of his home accompanied by family members. The Robinson local speciality, made to a secret recipe, was ginger wafer biscuits.

Robert Harris's nurseryman and florist shop, Beech Hill, decorated for the coronation of Edward VII, 1902. 'Mr. Harris covered the whole of the front of his house and shop with rustic work tastefully ornamented with flowering plants. There were festoons over the doorway with hanging baskets.'

George Brown's photographer's shop and studio at No. 24 Beech Hill, Westgate, *c.* 1922. The son of the Revd G.H. Brown, Congregational Minister, George junior was a perceptive photographer of local life during the early twentieth century. The young Laurence Pickles, apprenticed to Brown, was to carry on his skills.

Harold Stephenson's Motor Chara Co. of No. 16 Westgate advertised tours during the 1920s. This vehicle is probably the 2½-ton, eighteen-seater Guy of July 1921, which was later taken over by Barrett & Thornton buses.

Women war workers outside William Dawson & Sons' Ashfield Works, Westgate, 1914–18. This was the site that some sixty years earlier had produced the first 'Wharfedale' machine then named 'our own kind'.

Dawson & Sons' Ashfield Foundry floor, *c.* 1920. After the upheavals of war work, a basis had been found for combining three of the original Otley companies under the name of Dawson, Payne & Elliott Ltd in 1921.

Waite & Saville Ltd, Falcon Works, Burras Lane, *c.* 1898. This durable branch of the Otley engineering family tree was founded by Fred Waite after leaving Dawson's in 1892. Within a short time Waite had moved from his first Falcon Works in Station Road and started the development of the Burras Lane site, which operated independently until 1966. The production of the famous Falcon Platen press was supplemented by gravure, litho and rotary offset machines; stationers' technology included die-stamping, cornering, washering, punching and labelling machinery. Otley's trade with the colonies and wider world markets is well recorded in the museum's documentary collection. A 1928 agreement set up three travellers for the whole of South and Central America: 'Mr. Schrader will cover Colombia to Honduras, the Dominican Republic to Nicaragua.' A war report of 1945 records a doubling of the workforce and continuous working with night shifts exceeding seventy-five hours weekly. Waite & Saville were near the very end of a prolific line of Otley's industrial revolutionaries.

GUY CROFT IRON WORKS,

OTLEY, YORKSHIRE. Dec 3rd 187

The Committee of Otley Mechanics Institute

TO JAMES EXLEY & SON,

WHITESMITHS AND BELL-HANGERS.

PALISADING.

IRON AND WIRE FENCING
OF EVERY DESCRIPTION.

ENTRANCE & FIELD GATES.

Hot Water Apparatus
AND
KITCHEN RANGES.

EVERY DESCRIPTION OF
PLAIN & ORNAMENTAL
WROUGHT AND CAST
IRON WORK

IRON ROOFING,
GIRDERS & COLUMNS.

BRASS CASTINGS, &c.

The output of Exley's Guy Croft Iron Works is illustrated here on an 1875 bill for an iron palisade at the Mechanics' Institute. The business had expanded to meet the demands for Victorian ornamental ironwork. William Exley's name-plate can still be seen on the Kirkgate church gates.

'The Procession', Westgate, 1907. The largest Otley street demonstration was that of the Friendly Societies. Their 1905 procession had forty-four floats or entries, in eleven classes.

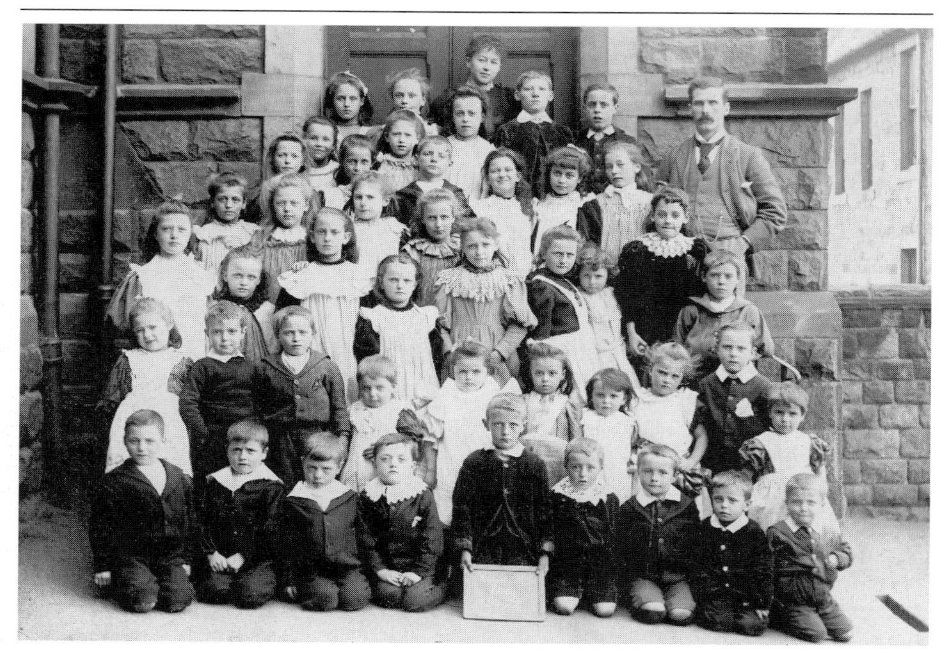

Westgate Board School, *c.* 1897. Margaret Blundell in charge of the Infants Department recorded that, despite the continuing measles epidemic, 'some improvement has been effected'.

Robinson's library and newsagents in Ashfield Place, a continuing focal point for the inhabitants to the west of the town, *c.* 1936. Robinson also had branches on Gay Lane and Farnley Lane. In the 1930s Robinson advertised his lending library of 4,000 volumes, beautiful picture postcards of the whole district, guidebooks and an up-to-date stock of music. 'Don't argue, we sell the things that make you happy, everything for your pleasure – always at your service.'

Western Otley from the Chevin, May 1887. The nucleus of Ackroyd's Mill provided considerable employment in worsted spinning, with the linear terraces stretching out to meet it from Westgate. The fashionable row of Ashfield Place stands out at the junction of Ilkley Road. Across the river is Ashfield House and the rural seclusion of the Weston Hall estate. Weston, Askwith and Denton moors stretch to the horizon, with the haze of the Washburn watershed in the far distance.

Duncan's Mill, *c.* 1907. Pegholme Mill, built between 1888 and 1891 to plans by Milnes & France, architects of Bradford, was a monument to local craft and industry. Maston (mason), Patrick (joiner), Chaffer (plasterer), Thornton (slater), Bennett (painter) and Burley (plumber) pieced it together, and Robinson provided fifty window blinds. The summary bill to William Ackroyd & Co. was £10,989 0*s* 7*d*.

Duncan's Mill weir, *c.* 1907. Ackroyd's worsted mill in 1825 was described as 'commanding the whole power of the Wharfe'. The flood plain of Mickle Ing to the west was the scene of constant dispute between landowners. The weir was cited by the highway authority in 1930 as the cause of constant flooding and was finally demolished in 1962.

The lodge gates for Westbourne House, the home of Thomas Arthur Duncan JP, proprietor of Otley Mills, *c.* 1907. The house was built for William Ackroyd, his will listing two gatekeepers' houses and the private road linking Bradford and Skipton turnpike roads. Mrs Duncan advertised for a strong stable boy here in April 1907.

Westbourne House, *c.* 1905. The ladies of the Congregational church, Bridge Street, visit the home of their patron. The photograph is inscribed: 'With best wishes for a happy Christmas & a bright New Year from A.M. Duncan.'

Hawthornden, Henry Dacre's villa in Bradford Road, *c.* 1900. The Hawthornden Brass Band, formed in 1890, had been the musical force behind the foundation of Dacre's Recreation Hall venture in Church Lane. Built in 1895, the 'Rec' later housed a theatre, winter garden, skating rink, billiard room, rifle-range, reading room and an arcade.

The Hawthornden Band, *c.* 1895. It performed in the recreation ground bandstand for 1*d* admission on concert nights and 3*d* for gala and special fêtes.

The Japanese Gardens, Otley Recreation Hall, *c.* 1895. Members could enjoy rustic seats, a summerhouse, a fountain and alfresco entertainment.

Jenny Slater as Britannia at the 'Rec', *c.* 1912. As young Jenny Blackburn she did much toing and froing up and down the Chevin from the family farm and café at Jenny's cottage. She vividly recalled her parts in such productions as *Bluebell in Fairyland*, *Tattercoats* and *The Goose Girl*.

Henry Dacre died suddenly in 1913; the writer of an appreciation shortly before had observed that the Recreation Hall without Mr Dacre would be like Wharfedale without the river. His old friend Albert Walker, counteracting the local gossip that Mr Dacre had been filling his pockets, said: 'His object was never the making of money; his death is a misfortune of the first magnitude. It was a dramatic finish to a dramatic life, one which has certainly not been paralleled in the history of Otley.'

Forrest Villas, Bradford Road, *c.* 1908. 'Gladys, her mother and Auntie' are said to be walking down the road to the Atkinson's house on the left.

Duncan Avenue, Bradford Road. The Urban Council's 'Westbourne Suburb' scheme of 1928 was instigated by the need to rehouse those displaced by clearances in Leeds Road, a waiting-list and also the demand for a rented home near work.

Bobbin Mill, Ellar Ghyll, *c.* 1908. The wooded ravine to the west of Otley known as West Gill supported four water-powered mills on the steeply falling Gill Beck. Cotton, woollen, flax and worsted mills worked here from the late eighteenth century onwards. Charles Hargreaves, master bobbin maker, held this mill and cottages during the mid-nineteenth century. At the time of the photograph J. Hinchcliffe worked the mill.

High Mill, Ellar Ghyll, *c.* 1906. In the 1790s the site was described as 'the Cotton Water Mill at Oaks Farm, millwrights Work and going gear'. This mill was insured by Marshall of Leeds and William Mounsey of Otley, hosiers and cotton spinners.

Otley station, *c.* 1910. While the line of the branch railway of 1865 is familiar, the unsuccessful plans made between 1845 and 1859 are not. How different would the market town have been with the iron road crossing at Otley Bridge or the Cross Pipes Inn, Westgate? The Otley stations that might have been exist only in the archives.

The end of the line: Otley station, 1966. 'Tomorrow late in the afternoon, the last passenger train will emerge from Bramhope Tunnel and swing into the down branch platform at Arthington,' wrote the *Wharfedale Observer* on Friday 19 March 1965. 'So tomorrow farewell!'

Otley Chevin from the station footbridge, *c.* 1905. On 12 May 1859 John William Brown, the Otley naturalist, had recorded in his diary: 'A warm south-east breeze and the sun shining. All nature rejoicing! The cry cuckoo! cuckoo! resounds from the woods on Chevin side.'

Otley's oologist, Ike Thomas, took Chevin cuckoos' eggs from the nests of meadow pipits in 1934. Thomas added the eggs of Chevin magpie, woodcock, pied wagtail, woodlark, garden warbler and pied flycatcher to his specimen cabinet. He amassed 438 eggs from 150 species between 1883 and 1938. On 8 May 1886 he was lowered 72 ft down Bempton cliffs on Flamborough Head to obtain a guillemot's egg, 'An experience I shall never repeat.'

Chevin steps, *c.* 1910. 'At the summit is Jenny's Hill cottage, where the visitor will find every accommodation to meet his bodily needs and to refresh him after his stiff pull up the hill. An excellent tea is provided for the modest outlay of 8d . . . or with ham and eggs 1s 6d. Mr Blackburn is skilled in the art of catering, and he is accustomed to providing for large parties.'

Surprise View and Jenny's Cottage, Otley Chevin, *c.* 1910. 'The summit is 925 feet above sea level, to the east on a clear day, the distant towers of York Minster can be discerned.'

The Royal Silver Jubilee beacon on Otley Chevin, May 1935. The fire was lit by a ceremonial torch carried to Surprise View by a relay of Scouts.

The Wharfedale Union smallpox hospital, south of Yorkgate in the township of Guiseley, *c.* 1946. The Joint Isolation Hospital was at Menston, later becoming the Wharfedale Children's Hospital.

Chevin Hall, the North Western Co-operative Convalescent Home, *c.* 1905. 'Carriages are in attendance at the station to convey visitors to the home which has a magnificent panorama of Wharfedale.'

The Yorkshire Clarion Holiday Club House and Camp, Chevin End. Started in 1902 with five second-hand bell-tents, in 1914 it was advertising a view of twenty miles of hill and dale – the Switzerland of England. 'Are you fed up with the bustle of Mudpool, the insipid gaieties of Sloshton and the tinsel delights of Borecambe?'

Mrs Hird at Yorkgate Farm, East Chevin Road, *c.* 1910. A series of short-term agreements between local quarrymen and the Hird family was typical of the piecemeal delving for Chevin stone that continued for generations. Between 1891 and 1898 the Hirds gave fixed-term rights to William Clapham, quarryman, and William and Thomas Maston of Otley. The Maston's building work in the district is graphically recorded in their account book for the second half of the nineteenth century.

William Flesher & Sons at Haw Lane quarries, Yeadon, *c.* 1910. The larger-scale nineteenth-century extractions of stone from the underlying strata were aided by steam crane. At this time Fleshers were also at Moor quarry, Guiseley.

The massive quarrying of Chevin stone at Pool Bank, 1959. Ernest Longfield of Otley came to work as a 'nipper' in 1924 for Whitaker & Sons. There were four stone planing machines, two frame saws, a compressed air drill, a steam crane and a derrick. Ernest collected Chevin bracken for packing stone to be transported in Sentinel steam wagons.

Bar House, Pool Bank. Chevin stone had a market in nineteenth-century docks, harbours and the foundations of public works. From 1880 stone was carried down a railway incline to be crane-loaded at Pool station. The line was not used after the First World War and the bridge was removed for scrap in 1941.

Otley, *c.* 1930. 'Visit picturesque and historic Wharfedale; Otley is the metropolis of the district. Access may be obtained by train, motor, tram or omnibus. The health-giving properties of its moorland air are unrivalled in Yorkshire. Its housing scheme is a model and there are many facilities in a large pleasure park.'

'Ring-a-ring-a-roses' in Manor Parade Gardens, *c.* 1910. The Council's first modest riverside park was acquired in 1909. 'Seats were placed there, and flowers and shrubs planted for the enjoyment of inhabitants and visitors.' Plots of allotment land on the north bank were bought between 1914 and the major scheme of 1923.

On the ice at Otley Bridge, 17 February 1929. The frozen Wharfe was the subject of a series of photographs by George Brown of Westgate. Describing skating on the river in the mid-nineteenth century, Brown's father chose Christopher Newstead as ice champion. 'His length of leg gave him advantage and his speed and manoeuvres were a marvel to us boys.'

The bowling green, Wharfemeadows, *c.* 1925. The park was laid out by the Urban Council in 1924 on land given by Major Fawkes of Farnley Hall. 'Bowls – Crown Green. Charges: – 4 players 2d each per hour.'

Wharfemeadows, *c*. 1926. 'Facilities for children include a sandpit and large paddling pool, together with see-saws and swings. Ample shelter is provided close to the children's playground.' Frank Cliffe's refreshment kiosk is in the centre distance.

The sandpit and children's corner, *c*. 1926. The pleasure grounds had open-air baths, six tennis courts and a nine-hole putting-green. The Pickles family had a fleet of fine new river boats, charging 9*d* per hour for one person and 6*d* each for two or more.

Bridge End in the great flood of 16 February 1935. Described as a Noah's Ark, but without livestock, the new auction mart floated on the flood plain. The contractors, F.W. Barker of Otley, saw their planking and building materials swept downstream. Rising and falling 10 ft in twenty-four hours, the river caused heavy damage to stock, land and property.

A family stroll along the sandbeds, photographed by W. Weegmann, *c.* 1905. A local guide extols the beauties of this route: 'The train might be taken to Arthington, then proceed along the highroad to Pool, cross the Bridge, and take the first turn on the left. After visiting Leathley, return to Farnley Park Lodge, and walk along the Sandbeds to Otley. About four miles.'

Building bridges across the Wharfe with Otley and Ilkley Companies of the Royal Engineer Volunteers, 19 May 1902.

Otley Company 2nd West Yorkshire Royal Engineer Band in camp at Redcar, 1903. Colonel Child, addressing the parents of Otley many years earlier on the first inspection of their 'citizen defenders', had urged them not to be under the erroneous impression that the volunteer movement would have a demoralising influence on their sons.

The 4th West Riding Howitzer Brigade in camp at Redcar, August 1908. Addressed to Miss Alice Whitehead, No. 2 South Parade, Otley, the card message reads: 'some of our lot cleaning harness in camp, we are having very warm weather here, enjoying myself in the pink.' Ten years later many of their successors would be lost in the grey mud of France.

The 'Otley lads' of the West Riding Howitzer Brigade have made themselves a home-from-home in a wooden hut named Chevin Villa. One local man recalled his distant memories of First World War soldiers marching down Leeds Road. 'I used to stand on the garden gate and shout Daddy! When they'd gone past and my Daddy hadn't come, I used to cry.'

10th Howitzers at the Mechanics' Institute, Otley. On Friday 11 June 1915 Eric Cowling – later founder of Otley Museum – returned from camp at Doncaster to be billeted in his home town. By the Sunday the institute was filled with recruits under Major Hall. 'No one gives him a good word.'

The Ancient Order of Foresters' float for the annual Friendly Societies' procession, 27 August 1910. Otley coal and lime merchant, J.T. Parnaby, stands by his wagon, which is harnessed to 'Little Prince'.

St John Ambulance Brigade. The brigade was formed on 14 November 1888, and the horse-drawn ambulance was presented to Otley by Colonel Dawson of Weston in 1889. First aid training was held at the Drill Hall.

The mammoth 'Old Otley' lantern-slide lecture of 1906 was given in aid of St John Ambulance funds under the chairmanship of patron Col. Dawson. Charles Walker showed 293 slides, with music being provided by the Otley Band and Hand Bell Ringers.

Section Two

WHARFEDALE

Milner Wood junction with Ilkley Moor beyond, c. *1950. The Midland Railway company's branch turned left to Menston. A Wharfedale excursion to Bolton Abbey via that station on Whit Monday 1950 cost* 2s 2d. *The last journey from Menston through Milner Wood was on 24 June 1965. Will rail travel ever pass this way again?*

Newall Hall, home of Thomas Clifton Wilkinson JP, principal landowner of Newall-with-Clifton, *c.* 1890. Edmund Barker's seventeenth-century home, walled garden and summer-house had been purchased in 1758 by John Ward, attorney. He redeveloped the site, diverted the road and enlarged the gardens. The property was inherited by Thomas Clifton and Francis Billam and then passed on to the Wilkinsons.

Newall Carr Road, *c.* 1890. 'Newhall is a small village. Some of the cottages have been lately unroofed. It has the ungracious garb of desolation. The hamlet of Clifton is scattered under the edge of a common of ling called Newhall Carr.' So writes an observer in the early nineteenth century. In the centre is Dawson's farm and on the right Newall Old Hall.

Newall Old Hall, the much dismembered medieval mansion of the Keighley family, *c.* 1885. 'The riches of its ancient splendour removed; and decay has destroyed its plantations and gardens.'

Newall Old Hall, rear elevation, *c.* 1908. J.M.W. Turner made a watercolour of a porch here before its removal by his friend Walter Fawkes in 1814. Dated 1624, with fluted pillars, the doorway is now attached to Farnley Hall.

Dawson's farm, Newall, *c.* 1920. The farm included the house, barn, stables, mistals, back garth, fold yard, stack garth, gardens and limekiln. Newall Old Hall stands forlorn on the right with the central tower truncated. It was nearing the end of its long history, which came in 1925.

An artist's impression of the new Wharfedale Union Workhouse at Newall erected in 1873. The Guardians considered this site 'an elevated and healthy situation' providing for 100 inmates. The staff were to be: George Mellor (Master), the Revd Mr Anderson (Chaplain), Thomas Ritchie (Surgeon) and Mrs Mellor (Matron). On the right was the casual ward for vagrants and the admission gate.

Neddy Emmott, who was said to have been admitted to the Workhouse in 1874. He stayed some forty years and became a Newall personality, allowing his portrait to be used on postcards which raised one guinea for toys for Workhouse children. The Guardians sent the children to school in Otley, 'so that they will be accustomed to mix with other children and less liable to be permanently pauperised'.

The Workhouse main building, *c.* 1900. People used to say: 'He's gone to Otley Workhouse and he'll die 'cos they've given him a bath.'

Redlands, Billams Hill, *c.* 1920. The four groups of mock-Tudor villas were developed by Thomas Turnbull, solicitor, between 1905 and 1907. Fairbank & Wall of Manor Square were the architects.

Newall Carr Road and the corner of Weston Lane, *c.* 1925. The house on the right is Woodview built for £700 in 1898 by John Dickinson. He was registrar for Fewston, plans inspector for Wharfedale Rural District Council, and Timble diarist.

Belmont, Newall, *c.* 1880. Built for William Dawson before his death in 1876, perhaps this was the retirement villa that the founder of Otley's printing machine industry never enjoyed. This became the home of Thomas Duncan, worsted spinner of Duncan Barraclough and William Ackroyd & Co., Otley Mills. Duncan commuted from the north side of the river, and surely he could hardly imagine the later suburban expansion.

Ashfield House, *c.* 1880. The house was built by Jonathan Chadwick in about 1816 with funds from his father's estate. Chadwick was described at the time of his wedding in 1782 as a considerable maltster. The processing of barley for the local thirst was big business: 'The numerous maltkilns, the principal support of the town in those days, were busy to the utmost; fortunes were being made by many.' By the mid-1830s the fortune had been lost. The Revd Joshua Hart, in his lecture on Wharfedale, commented that Mr Chadwick had not counted the cost, for he was unable to finish. The estate was purchased by the Hartley family and became the home of John Walker Hartley JP. During the Second World War it was used as the North Eastern School of Wireless Telegraphy. Then history was repeated in 1948 when the house was purchased by Tetley's Brewery.

Farnley Hall, the home of Turner's patron, the late Walter Fawkes, 1830. On a visit here in 1884 John Ruskin remarked: 'Farnley Hall is a unique place – a place where a great genius was loved and appreciated, who did all his best work for that place.'

The Elizabethan façade of Farnley Hall. The hall was disfigured by fragments seized from other houses on the Fawkes' estates. Visitors from Otley's Recreation Hall are posed around the original porch taken from Menston Hall, which was previously erected as a gateway to the Farnley flower garden.

Lake Tiny, Farnley Estate, *c.* 1900. 'Farnley Lake is beautifully embossomed in woodland between the Park and Washburn,' wrote Edmund Bogg in his *Two Thousand Miles in Wharfedale.* The lake was reached from the hall by the Woodwalk or Glen and was the subject of evocative watercolours by Turner.

Drum Head Service of the Northumberland Hussars, Farnley Park Camp, 1914.

Northumberland Hussars boxing in camp, Farnley Park, 1914.

Northern Command Schools, Farnley Camp, *c.* 1917. Eva Fox, assistant manageress on the catering staff, made photo and autograph albums of the visiting officers and men. The poignant autographs include a skilled cartoon by Stanley Holloway of the 4th Connaught Rangers, who is seated in the middle row, second from right.

Gas and Bombing Schools, Farnley Camp. Lt. Sydney Stevens of 1st London Regiment signed this card: 'Yours till hell freezes.' 'If you know a better 'ole than Otley, go to it,' comments Murray Asher of the Seaforth Highlanders.

The John Carr wing of Farnley Hall, which was begun in 1786. The cross in the window notes the birth of 'Alwyn', and wartime use as a maternity hospital.

Weston Hall, the Elizabethan house of the Vavasour family, *c.* 1895. This sylvan estate is the veiled setting for *The Rose of Wharfedale*, a novel by Albert Walker, featuring the blue-eyed auburn-haired Rose Granton, the sweetest flower of Wharfedale.

'The Isinglass shooting party' at Eastwood cottages, 6 September 1893. Weston Hall lost lands to the new Weston Manor estate after partition in 1885. No doubt moorland game covets supplied the shooting party.

Joseph England, gamekeeper, Weston Hall, and his wife Mary, 1908. England came to the formerly mantrapped estate in 1855 when it was described as rich with every description of game: grouse, pheasants, partridges, woodcocks, snipe, plovers, hares, rabbits, foxes, wild ducks and fish.

The earthwork bank and ditch below Wood Hall Lane at Clifton was not the site of Cromwellian belligerence, but was the machine-gun position for Otley's Home Guard on target practice.

The Roebuck Inn, Newall-with-Clifton, *c.* 1910. George Spence had the inn from 1852 to 1883, doing a good passing trade with the Washburn reservoir navvies during the 1870s. Competition for custom with the Traveller's Rest a few doors up, which opened in 1853, had led to their nicknames: 'Spite' and 'Malice'. Arthur Parker was the landlord in around 1910.

Askwith looking east, *c.* 1903. Describing the typical thatched cottages here a century earlier, a chronicler of Wharfedale states: 'The handsome buildings cannot illumine the dark shade of the miserable huts among which they are placed, whilst the contaminating gloom of the meaner habitations veils all the beauties of Asquith.'

Askwith looking west, at the junction of Moor Lane, *c.* 1905. On the left a cart stands outside Jim Rhodes' village smithy, which still retains a roadside hooping plate.

J. Hannam & Co., builders and contractors of Charles Street, Otley, putting the finishing touches to the new Askwith School in 1907. 'All kinds of Jobbing work neatly & promptly executed. Good workmanship guaranteed.'

The damstones at Greenholme Mill, Burley. On a postcard dated 1916, Ethel tells Ada: 'You will see that I am at Burley having a good time.' A century earlier Burley had been described as 'a delightful village, though contaminated physically and morally by a cotton mill'. Cotton manufacture ceased here in 1848 but water power continued.

Napier Wagon, William Fison & Co., Greenholme Mills, *c.* 1920. *Coming up Singing: local memories recorded in Otley Museum* recalls this mill transport. 'They used to put wooden seats on the motor lorries that they used for carrying coal or anything else.'

The demolition of the Fison family's Greenholme mansion in 1923. Erected in 1820, later that century the house and mill were at the nub of a large worsted industry dominating local employment and controlling the village. William Edward Forster was Fison's partner in the 1850 mill estate.

Caley Hall, the home of Henry Dacre who died here in 1913. In the mid-eighteenth century the hall passed to the Fawkes of Farnley, who developed the Chevin slopes as an exotic game park. Caley Crags provided a dramatic foreground to Turner's *Hannibal Crossing the Alps*. The house was demolished in 1964.

Postmarked 'Pool 1913', this card shows the church, bridge, White Hart and village streets. The bottom view is outside Hanley's Croft Cottage, which offered refreshments, cycle repair, stabling, shoeing and general smith work.

The north portal of the Bramhope tunnel, *c.* 1905. The Leeds & Thirsk Railway Act received Royal Assent on 21 July 1845, heralding the invasion of the railway age into Wharfedale. The tunnel workings were over 2 miles long, 25 ft high and, at their deepest point, 290 ft under a trembling village. At the height of the excavations 2,300 navvies and 400 horses were employed. The working shafts through sandstone and shale were subject to continuous floods. Into the darkness went the tunnel tigers of subterranean Bramhope and their supporting labourers: the nippers, tippers, spraggers and wagon men. A mile further north, off a towering embankment, were masons perched 80 ft over the river on the twenty-one arches of the new Wharfedale viaduct. The grim catalogue of casualties is commemorated in the Otley churchyard memorial (see page 8).

Bramhope Hall lodge, *c.* 1890. The original drive opposite Church Hill was blocked by the new turnpike road embankment some fifty years earlier. The new lodge and gates were surmounted by the Rhodes family acorn, the same device appearing on the altar front of the Puritan chapel.

The good people of Bramhope celebrate the coronation of Edward and Alexandra around the village cross, 9 August 1902.

Castley Hall, rebuilt by Robert Dyneley *c.* 1700. The site has revealed interesting features including cruck timbers from an earlier building, an eighteenth-century privy and a large bedroom mural of a hunting scene.

Arthington Nunnery farm, *c.* 1900. Built on the site of the original Cluniac Priory, the farm was the home of the Yeadon family. The fact that William Dawson, Otley's nineteenth-century machinist, was indebted to landed investment, is contained in the words: 'The infant industry was weak on its legs, Mr Yeadon gave it nourishment and thus strengthened it went forward on its prosperous ways.'

Otley island platform at Arthington, *c.* 1905. The original station on the line was on Arthington Lane, serviced by horse-bus three times daily from Otley. There were objections from Mr Darwin of Creskeld on the more southerly siting of the new station. The first train to Otley stopped here at 7.26 a.m. on 1 February 1865; the passengers waited in a wooden shed.

This card, postmarked 'Arthington village 1911', was sent to Miss Whitfield in Harrogate, 'love Whiskers'. Arthington viaduct was the scene of more tragic events in 1847 when two workmen fell 80 ft to their deaths in the River Wharfe.

The isolated church of St Mary at Stainburn, *c.* 1910. Formerly in the old parish of Kirkby Overblow, the church remains a classic landmark of change in the countryside. The suggestion of Scandinavian settlement, medieval monastic sheep farming from Fountains Abbey, and subsequent depopulations, leave the shadows of lost souls in the surrounding pastures.

Stainburn School, *c.* 1910. The children of the farming community had been educated in the village and at Leathley until the building of an 'infant school and teacher's house in the Elizabethan style in 1862 at the cost of Mr Fawkes'.

March Ghyll Reservoir outlet. In May 1902 Otley Urban Council cut the first sod of its new waterworks on Middleton Moor near Ilkley. The valve of the 6 mile pipeline was officially turned on by Mrs T.A. Duncan on 13 April 1907.

Otley Urban District councillors, officials and wives on their annual visit to March Ghyll during 1930. The trip involved an inspection of the works and valve tower, a farmhouse tea and a motor coach trip of beauty spots. One trip in 1921 noted that Otley had consumed 9,178,550,000 gallons of water since the supply opened!

Otley Camera Club with Mr W.H. Dawson in the grounds of Maple Grange, Ilkley Road. In 1909 the Camera and Art Society had club rooms at No. 3 Wesley Street and made many sorties into the local countryside.

A splendid view of the stepping stones at Bolton Priory captured by Otley photographer Harold Stephenson during an excursion up Wharfedale in the summer of 1905.

Section Three

WASHBURN VALLEY

River Washburn, Leathley, c. 1925. As a place of tranquillity, generations of ramblers have tramped up the riverside paths of the Washburn valley, catching a first tantalising glimpse of 'the Leeds lake district' through a woodland frame. For the older inhabitants of the valley, in the late nineteenth century, much of the timeless landscape had ceased to exist. The decay of village, mill and cottage, the desertion of ploughland and pasture and the gradual compulsory purchase of the whole watershed, was change too far.

St Oswald's Church, Leathley, *c.* 1900. The early Norman tower is described a century before as 'faced with the grey of rocks, scarcely one of which had received the tutoring chisel'. In front stand the old whipping-post and five-hole stocks 'for two an' a hawf pair o' legs'.

Leathley Almshouses, *c.* 1900. 'This is an elegant building, placed in the middle of the village. In the body there is a school for the education of poor children; the wings are separated for the occupation of widows and old womin.' The memorial stone of 1769 records the endowment of the Hitch family.

Leathley lodge and gatehouse, *c.* 1900. The Victorian mock-Elizabethan lodge design of the Fawkes estate is in contrast with the real surviving timber elements surveyed inside some of the Leathley houses.

Leathley bridge, *c.* 1900. This well-arched bridge, doubled in width, gave better access to Leathley after purchase by the Fawkes estate.

Leathley Hall, photographed by Israel Todd of Otley, *c.* 1890. The fine early eighteenth-century home of the Hitch family was described a century later as having the humble look of fallen grandeur. 'At present it is inhabited by a farmer, whose labourers unceremoniously enough perfume its costly chambers with the odours of the stable or cow house.'

Mill House, Leathley, *c.* 1920. With a Leathley mill mentioned in Domesday valued at 2*s*, perhaps this site holds its successor. The 14 ft wheel has gone, but the internal machinery survives.

Lindley Mill goit, *c.* 1905. The Lindley corn mill is depicted on a map of the boundaries of the Forest of Knaresborough in the late sixteenth century, and the site is still clear today.

Lindley Wood, *c.* 1910. The first of the Leeds Corporation reservoirs of the Washburn valley, Lindley was built between 1869 and 1875 as a compensation reservoir. The provision of clean Washburn water for the growing population of industrial Leeds, met with real hostility from landed proprietor Francis Fawkes of Farnley. In 1852 he referred to the proponents as 'the Leeds water pirates', one of whom was the Otley-born John Hope Shaw. Plans nevertheless went ahead on the Fawkes estates, and the navvy invasion of Lindley Wood was graphically recorded by the Revd Mr Evans, Rector of Leathley and founder of the Navvy Mission Society. The society's quarterly letter was edited by Mrs Elizabeth Garnett of Otley, who also gave a semi-fictional account of the scene in her navvy novel *Young Six Foot*. The navvies' village below Greystone Beck had thirty-five buildings including brick huts, a wooden church, beerhouse, store and a school which had to adapt as a smallpox hospital. On 6 October 1871 thirty cases of typhoid fever were reported among the reservoir builders. As the navvies moved up the Washburn to complete the reservoirs of Swinsty and Fewston beyond, Mrs Garnett was to tirelessly champion their cause until her death in 1921.

Bishopwood house, 1949. Traditionally held with the archbishops' Newall Old Hall estate at Otley, the sixteenth-century lease describes this as Northwoodhouse 'with the cutting of the holly and felling of ten oak trees'. An earlier timber house was replaced in stylish stone by George Newsome in 1737. In an act of pure twentieth-century vandalism, the house was later stripped of its façade leaving the stark gable ends and the barn standing.

Dob Park lodge in Mounsey's postcard series, *c.* 1910. Built on the upper moorland waste of Weston Parish by the Vavasours of Weston Hall around 1600, the 'Castle' was probably the centre of a deer park. By the late eighteenth century the lodge was a romantic ruin, which was sketched by Turner in about 1816.

Dob Park bridge, *c.* 1900. This high arch packhorse bridge was built in 1768 to replace a previous bridge destroyed in a flash flood.

Dob Park mill, *c.* 1910. 'The wheels silent and the miller has gone – 'tis now a place of memories.' A tiny chap-book, entitled *Aunt Jane's Tales* and used by the Thornton family who lived here, records poignant family details. '1841 August 23 Elizabeth Thornton. First Began To Walk by Thomas Sutell millwright. Cured her with 6d of Swallows Oile. She was 5 years 1 month 3 weeks 5 Days before she cud walke by her Self.'

The road at Norwood Edge, *c.* 1925. The boundaries of Lindley, Farnley and Norwood lie concealed under the waters of Lindley Reservoir at the old ford of Lippers Wath. On the right is Lindley Wood rising to Hopkinson Gill and Norwood Edge Plantation at 950 ft. On the left is Norwood Bottom, Norwood Hall and the new chapel under construction.

A Washburn family gathering at Norwood Bottom, one of the groups of scattered farmsteads throughout the township, *c.* 1900.

Norwood Hall. This fine late seventeenth-century house was photographed in around 1900 for Henry Mounsey's Otley postcard series.

The Wesleyan Methodist chapel, Norwood Edge. The chapel was designed and illustrated by Oswald Homes, the Otley architect. The laying of the foundation stone took place on 26 August 1925 at 3 o'clock; tea in the marquee was at 4.30 p.m. and a public meeting was held at 7 p.m. Special Barrett & Thornton buses ran from Bondgate, Otley, to Norwood for a single fare of 9*d*.

The Sun Inn, Brame Lane, Norwood, *c.* 1905. Norwood township meetings were held here dealing with poor and highway rates, overseers, pinders, constables, repair of highways and letting of lanes. A little local difficulty was minuted on 19 November 1874 when Thomas Marston 'late surveyor' had failed to deliver up £4 19*s* lane money.

Craggs Mill, Norwood, *c.* 1920. Situated just south of Worstall Craggs, the mill was run by the Barker family for over a century. Powered by Spinksburn Beck, water was held in a millpond and weir below Wydra bridge and channelled on to an iron wheel. The mill was famed for its oatmeal, the Washburn's staple crop, and William Isaac Barker was miller here before its demolition in 1936.

Scow Hall, Norwood, *c.* 1950. Described as 'probably the oldest of the old halls of the valley of the Washburn; it also exhibits most symptoms of ruin and decay'. The home or property of the Beckwith, Breary, Fairfax, Wilkinson and Fawkes families and numerous tenant farmers, the hall was taken into the 'capacious maw' of the Leeds Corporation in 1900. It was badly neglected, but was finally listed as of architectural interest in 1957.

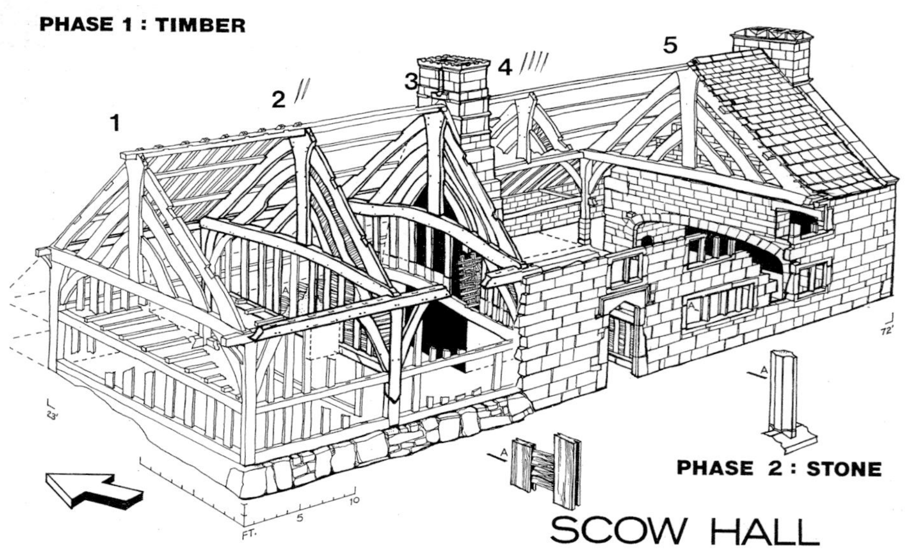

Architectural detail of Scow Hall by Paul Wood, 1980. The author's research and reconstruction between 1978 and 1988, revealed the frame assembly of the late medieval hall and its later stone cladding. The renewal of oak timbers and re-carving of stone elements on site were based on this survey.

Ling Cottage, Stainburn Moor, *c.* 1890. The contrast between the high-status Washburn houses like Scow Hall and the now-demolished Ling Cottage is clear. Located just outside the township boundaries of Norwood and Lindley Moor near Little Almscliff, the cottage's setting suggests its origins as a shepherd's hut or squatter's cottage on the moor edge. With adjoining boulder outcrops quarried as rubble walling and a roof of heather and sods, the house stood among bleak 800 ft pastures and had expansive views of moorland to the north. The aptly named Wonderful House stood a short distance to the west.

Fewston church, *c.* 1900. Rebuilt in 1697 after a fire, the pitch of the old thatch-roofed church can be seen on the tower. Beyond is the vicarage, enlarged by the Revd John Gwyther in 1867, and badly affected by landslip. Otley naturalist, John Brown, was here on 27 July 1857 when he collected caterpillars of 'the beautiful Vapourer moth'.

Fewston village, *c.* 1900. Fewston Parish had included the scattered hamlets of Blubberhouses, Norwood and Thruscross with the larger village of Timble Great. At the end of a major phase of waterworks depopulation, the village houses still show their ancient character scattered in irregular garths on the steep valley side.

Benson House, Fewston, *c.* 1879. As the massive upheavals of the Leeds Corporation reservoirs of Swinsty and Fewston drew to a conclusion, the resulting desolation at Fewston village was photographed by Israel Todd of Otley. By 1880 there were only eight families left in the 'ruined village'. Landowners were in dispute with the city aldermen about liability; the collapse had become a sad, public spectacle. While the undermining of the lower slopes was clearly damaging, the truth seems partly to lie with the builders of the village, 'who had an eye more to the picturesque than the solid, for they placed many of the houses on a continuously acting landslip. Some of the houses near the upper margin of the moving mass, are cracked from top to bottom, and twisted out of shape from the same cause.' Not only did the process of collapse cause human migration from the Washburn valley, but decaying buildings were transported for construction work elsewhere. The crumbling Crag Hall at the end of Busky Dyke Lane, formerly the home of the Parkinson family, was removed and re-erected stone by stone at Holly Hill, Huby, in 1957.

Hill Top, Fewston, *c.* 1920. Of these three dwellings only the house on the end of Busky Dyke Lane remains. The low seventeenth-century house on the left concealed earlier timber framing.

Meagill Lane Cemetery chapel. After the initial deputation to the Leeds Waterworks Committee in 1898 on the closure of Fewston churchyard, John Dickinson, Registrar for Fewston, did not report real progress until 1907. The new burial ground was opened on 30 September 1908. Dickinson himself was interred here in July 1912 after torrential rain had delayed his burial for two days.

Swinsty Hall, Little Timble, *c.* 1920. This small detached township of the York Archbishops' estates dates from the pre-Conquest period. Surrounded by the Forest of Knaresborough, the two farms at Nether Timble and Swinsty Hall itself, are the only remaining houses on the ancient manorial holding. The museum's Bramley family estate papers for Swinsty Hall tell of the lives of the Woods, Robinsons and Bramleys between 1575 and 1917. A marriage settlement of 1576 determines the building of 'a convenient house at Swinsty Hall'. The subsequent division of houses between old and new halls suggests completion of the main hall during the early seventeenth century. Henry Robinson of Old Laund not only brought the prosperity of woollen textiles to Swinsty in his 'shopp', but also some of the fine architectural fashions of the Lancashire Pennines to the new house. To the north of Swinsty Hall – and alongside the Washburn – was New Hall, the home of Edward Fairfax, author of *A discourse of Witchcraft* in 1621. Fairfax's claim that his daughters Helen and Elizabeth were bewitched by six local women, was rejected at York Assizes on two occasions in 1622. Henry Robinson of Swinsty Hall was one of the petitioners in the women's defence.

Masons and carpenters working on the waterworks reconstruction of Swinsty Hall barn, 17 June 1902. The initials of their employers and the date of the work can still be seen on the keystone of the arch.

'A' company of the Otley Home Guard take time off from sabotage duty at Swinsty Reservoir pipeline during the 1940s.

Washburn Valley Tenant Farmers' Show at Timble, 1908. At the show the farming fraternity met old friends, bemoaned the weather and waterworks rents, and compared the price of livestock. Animals were driven to and fro across Snowden Moor to Otley Market in all weathers.

Farm at Gill Becks, Timble, *c.* 1900. Commenting on the decay of his beloved valley in 1980, the late John Liddle of Stainburn commented: 'The Washburn valley has been destroyed first by Leeds Corporation and now by the Water Authority. They should have treasured the valley and preserved it, and they have destroyed it in every direction, which is the biggest sin I can think of. Those lovely smallholdings, the moment they get one empty – down with it.' This farm is now a pile of rubble and rotting timber.

Peat cutters, Washburn watershed, *c.* 1925. Turf Moor, Blubberhouses, records an important turbary in the upper valley. The extractive industry is also recorded in stone quarries, charcoal and limekilns, and attempts at lead mining as far south as Kex Gill.

A summer evening at Blubberhouses, *c.* 1920. This was the rural setting for the huge Westhouse flax mill, which stood here from the late eighteenth century, employing 300 workers including pauper apprentices. The mills, Skaife Hall and the Frankland Arms fell to the waterworks, while the post office was victim to road widening in 1969.

St Andrew's Church, Blubberhouses, *c.* 1910. The church was erected at the expense of Lady Frankland Russell and consecrated by the Bishop of Ripon on 24 September 1856.

Blubberhouses Hall, *c.* 1905. Lady Frankland's grandson, Lord Walsingham, used the house in the late nineteenth century as a shooting lodge. In 1872 the adjoining heather moorland witnessed his notorious sporting prowess, when the good lord bagged 423 brace of grouse in fourteen hours.

Low Green, West End, with the post office and church, *c.* 1930. The township of Thruscross covers both the high watershed of the Washburn valley and the Forest of Knaresborough. It contained the hamlets of West End, Low Green, Thruscross Green and Bramley Head. The tributary waters of Capelshaw Beck met the Washburn at Beckfoot Bridge. With a Pennine tradition of farming and cottage textiles, and a factory system's search for upland water power, it was inevitable that even this remote valley would see the industrial revolution. Again it was a late eighteenth-century Otley connection that was to merge town with countryside, with the erection of a large cotton mill above Street Lane bridge. John Walker (silver plater), Joseph Hardcastle (grocer), Richard Holdsworth (maltster), Robert Thompson (joiner), and William Maude (ironmonger), all of Otley, were investors in the new factory. The early nineteenth century saw the erection of further mills, an influx of labour and a change to linen production. The secluded hive of industry was short-lived; the remoteness of markets and transport, and a general slump all heralded decline. By 1900 the deserted village of West End was already a legend. 'The hands that worked these once busy temples of industry, have long since departed to fresh scenes of labour in the large towns.'

The church and ruins of Patrick's mill, Low Green, West End, *c*. 1900. The photographer is W. McKenzie of Norwood.

Holy Trinity Church, Thruscross, *c*. 1910. Although the proposal to build a fourth reservoir at Thruscross was included in the Leeds Waterworks Act of 1867, the church finally disappeared under the new dam in 1966.

Bee boles at Thruscross, September 1953. The ruined mill in the valley, backed by conifer plantations, is seen from the rear of the Gate Inn and Horsman's Smithy, at the junction of Scot Lane and Ratten Row.

Rocking School, West End, *c.* 1945. This school was attended by the young John Liddle from Spittle Ings. John, born at Scaife Hall Farm, Blubberhouses in 1906, remembered: 'The playground was sand and with two pieces of wood we could make stone walls, fields, farm yards and live-stock, and we used to farm in the sand in the playground.'

West End Methodist chapel centenary, 1937. Built at the top of Clogger Lane, the chapel and its Sunday school were often full in the early years with dissenting members of the farming and factory communities.

The Stone House Inn, Thruscross, *c.* 1925. The end of the hospitable road for travellers between the lush valleys of the Wharfe and the Washburn and the bleak moorland of Greenhow. This book has tramped the same paths as the farming families to Otley market ten miles away, and from a distant horizon we first saw on a bright May day in 1887.

Acknowledgements

The author is grateful to the management committee of Otley Museum Trust for permission to publish this compilation of photographs. Thanks go to all museum friends who have donated items for the collection. The following local photographers are particularly acknowledged for their work shown here.

W. Barraclough • T.V. Benn • A. Blakey • W. Brockbank • G. Brown
Edson & Demain • J. Garratt • W. McKenzie • J. Marjoram • H. Mounsey
A. North • E. Patrick • L. Pickles • R. Scatchard • R. Shaw • H. Stephenson
I. Todd • C. Walker • W. Weegmann • T. Woodhead • E. Worsnop
and the unknown photographer

Contemporary and other descriptive quotations are taken from museum publications and documentary and primary sources in the collection. Limitations on space do not allow individual annotations. Readers wishing to pursue research enquiries should contact the keepers for specific references. *Otley Museum: a guide to the documentary collection* is available on request.